# GLORIA

**One-in-a-bar; firmly** ($\dot{}$ = 60 – 72)

Glo - ry God in the high - est, and peace to his peo - ple on earth. Lord God, heav'n - ly King, al - migh - ty God and Fa - ther, we wor - ship you, we give you thanks, we praise you for your glo - ry.

★ Omit small notes when the support of a choir is available.

Communion Service (S 598)

4

Communion Service (S 598)

*Harmony is optional and for choir only; congregation sing soprano line.

Communion Service (S 598)

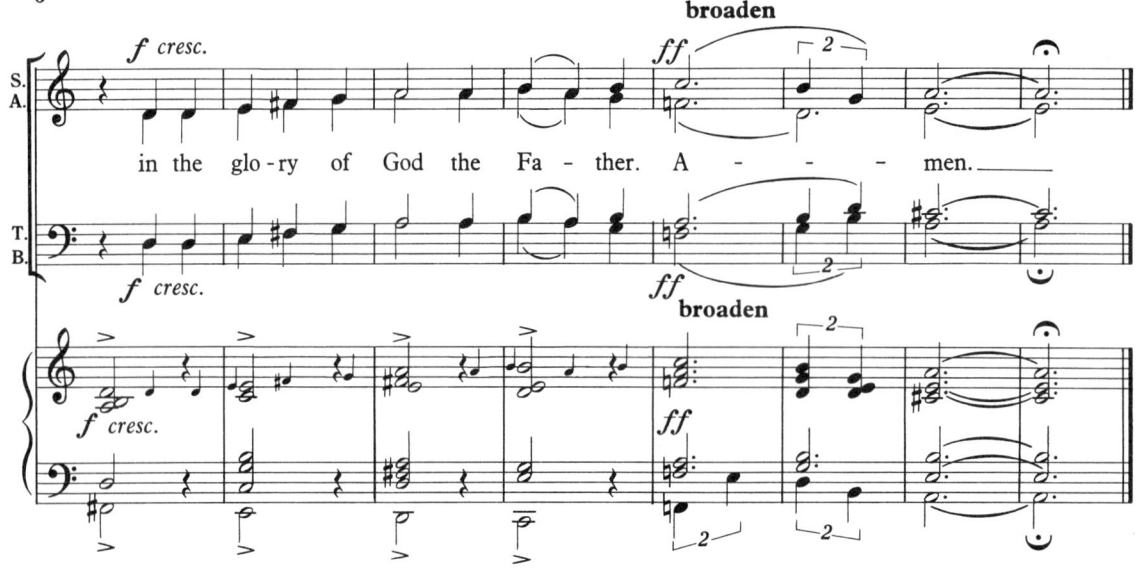

The Creed and the Lord's Prayer are to be said.

# THE GOSPEL

(Reader announces the Gospel)★

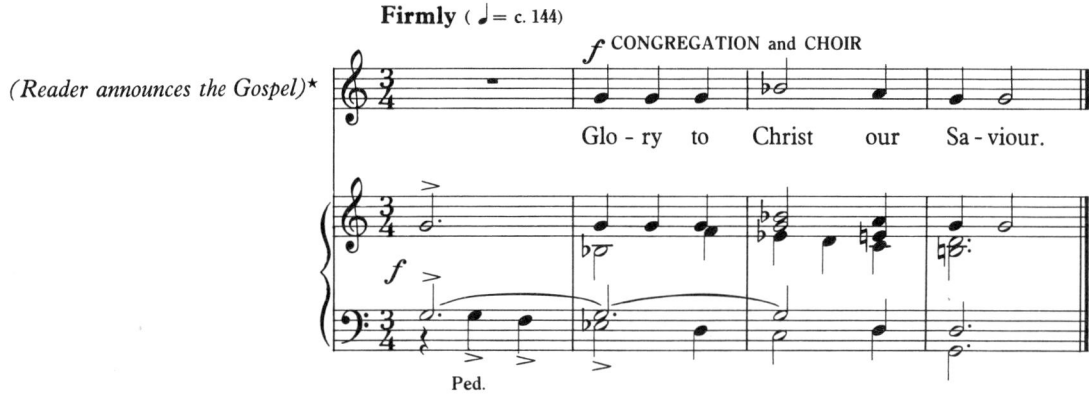

READER *(at the end of the Gospel):*
This is the Gospel of Christ.

★ It is preferred that the Gospel announcement, the Gospel, and the conclusion to the Gospel should be said. If they are intoned, the announcement and conclusion should be sung on G.

# SURSUM CORDA

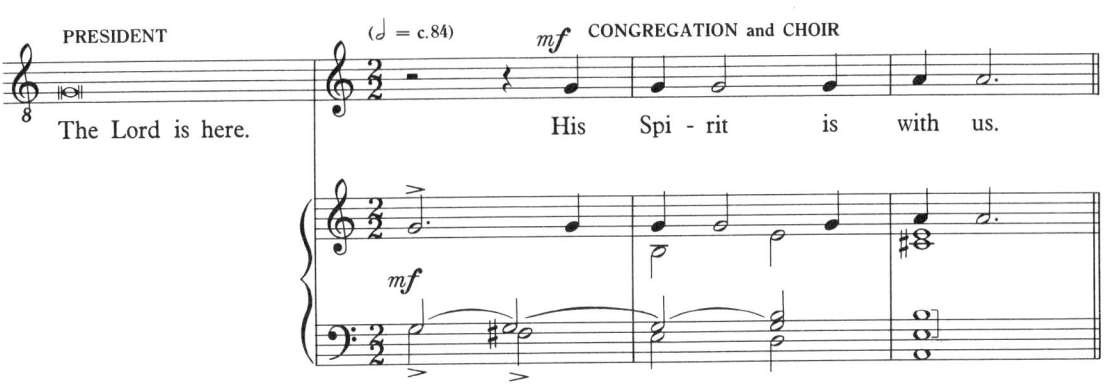

The words of the Thanksgiving which follow should be said and not intoned.

Communion Service (S 598)

# SANCTUS

President: . . . we proclaim your great and glorious Name,
for ever praising you and saying:

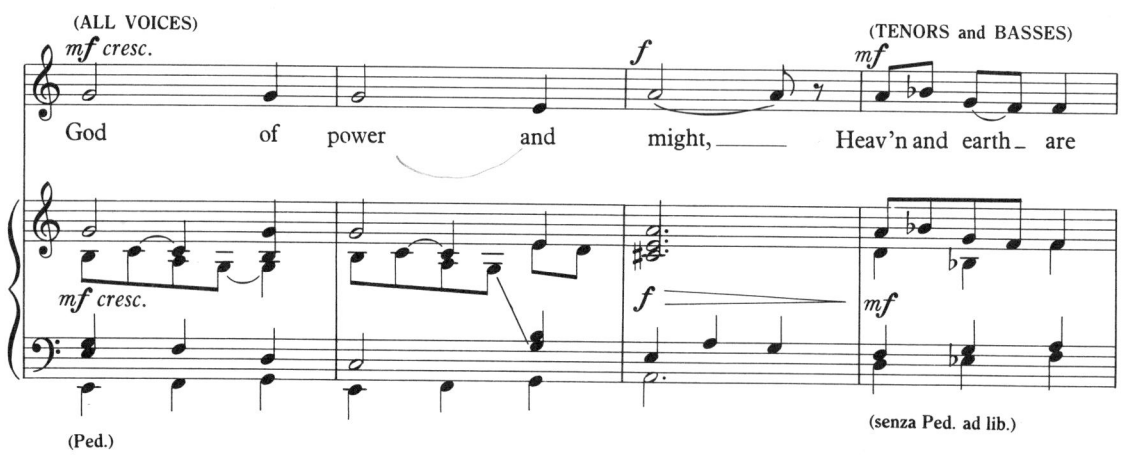

Communion Service (S 598)

# ACCLAMATIONS

President: . . . Do this, as often as you drink it,
in remembrance of me.

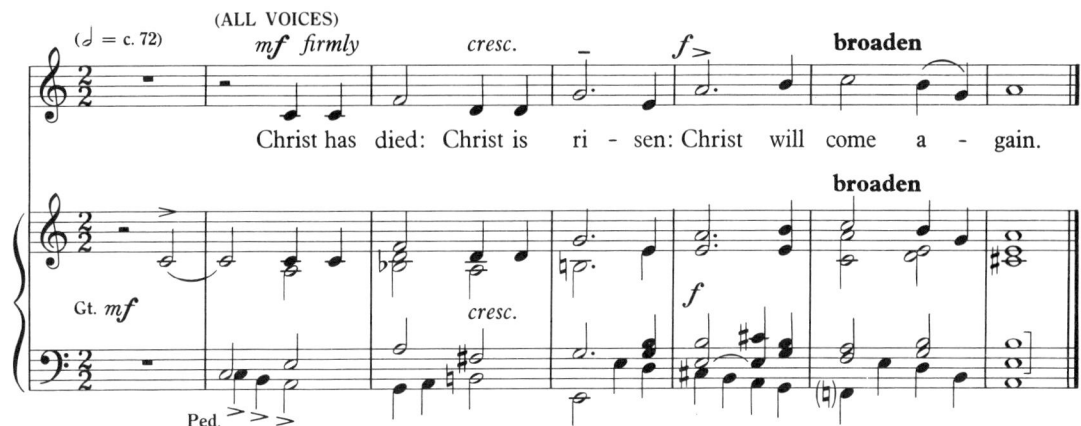

President: . . . we worship you, Father Almighty,
in songs of everlasting praise:

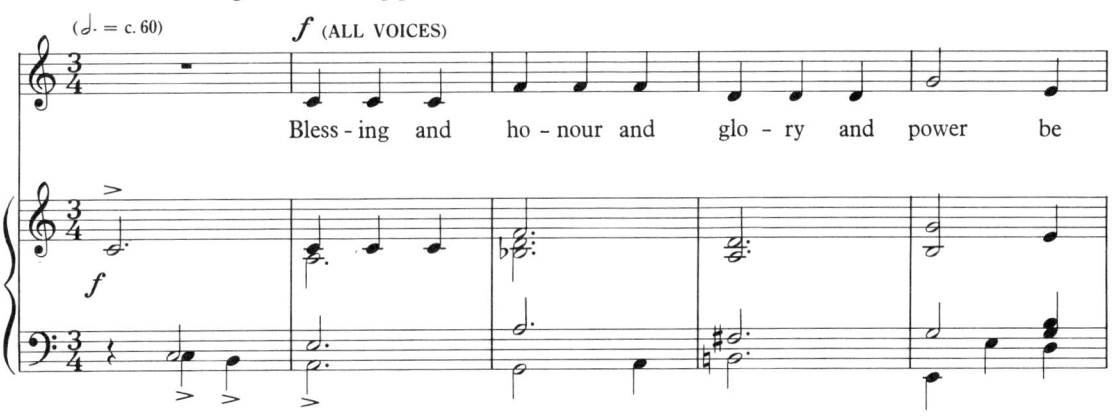

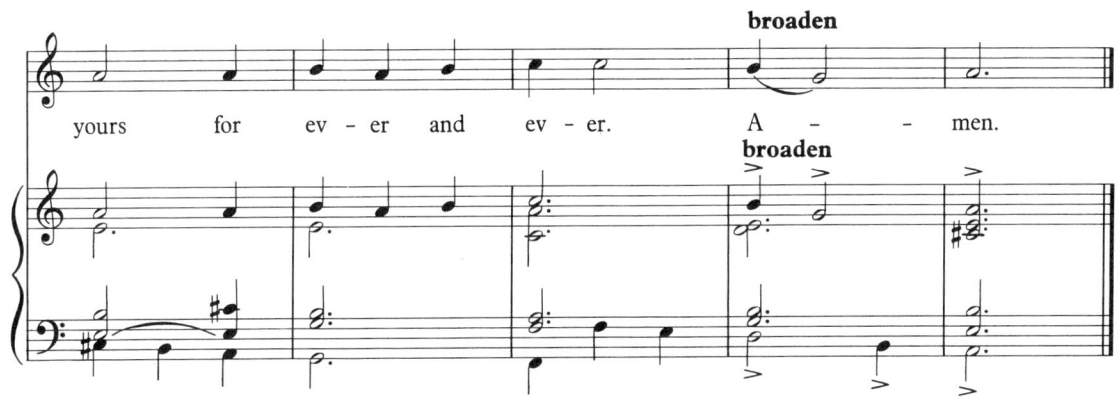

Communion Service (S 598)

## BENEDICTUS*

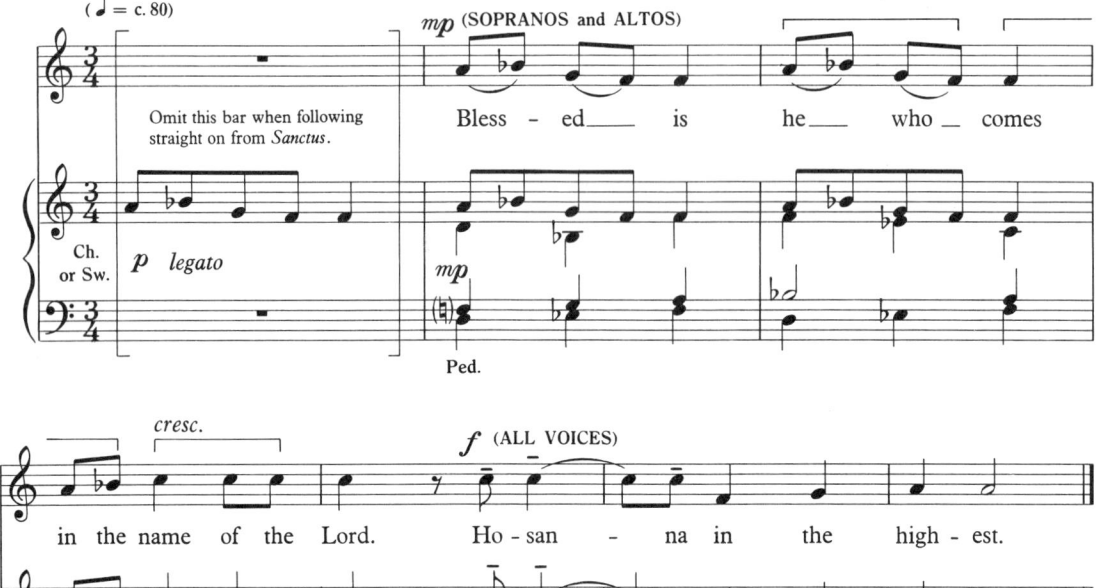

*This may be sung immediately following the *Sanctus* without a break, but it is preferred that it should be sung either directly before or after the breaking of bread, or else during the administration of Communion as an alternative to, or in addition to, the *Agnus Dei*.

## AGNUS DEI†

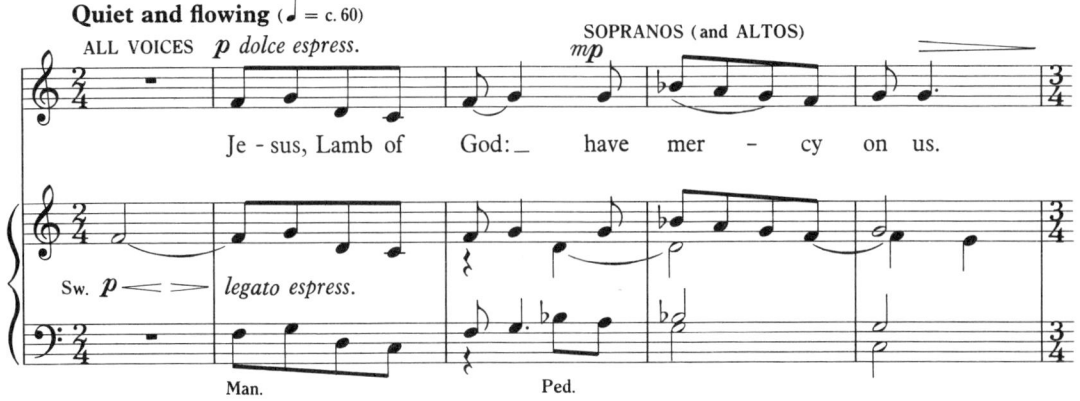

† Sung by choir only.

Communion Service (S 598)

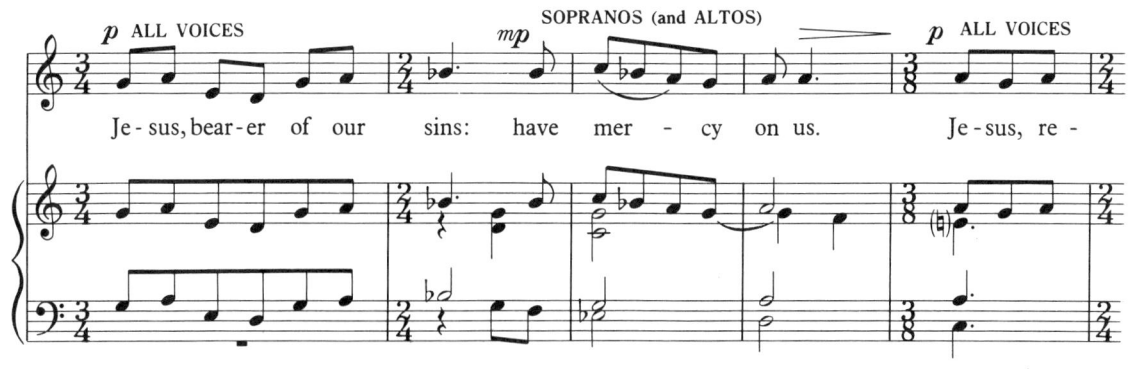

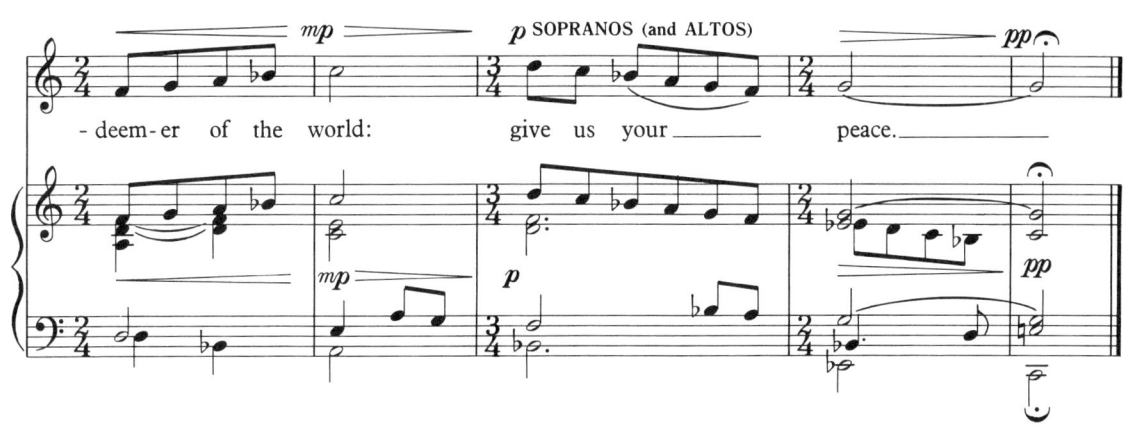

## DISMISSAL

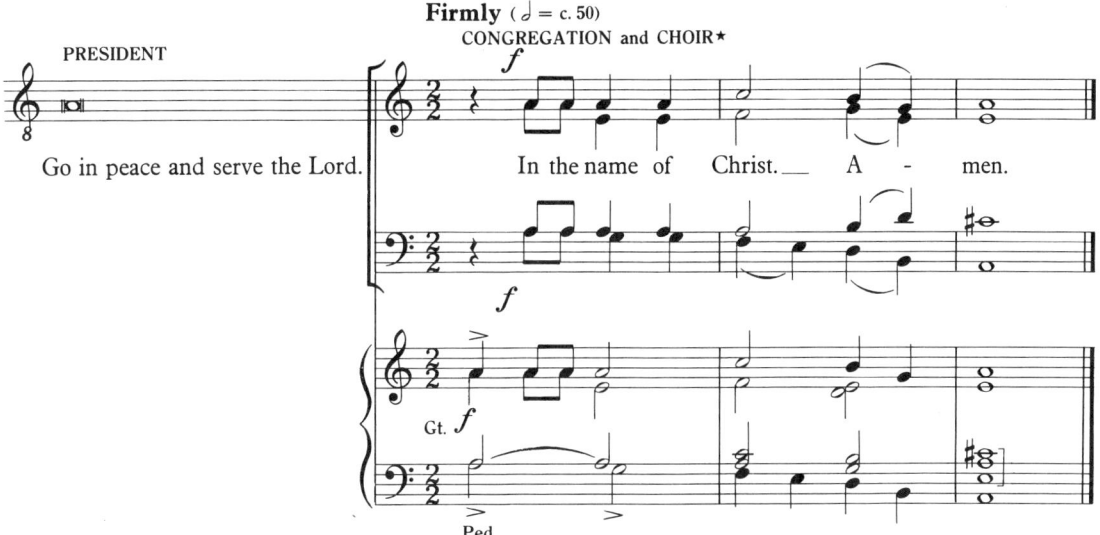

★ Here again harmony is optional and for choir only.

Communion Service (S 598)

S 598 Communion Service RUTTER

ISBN 0-19-351638-1